Can You Tell a SKINK from a SALAMANDER?

Anna Claybourne

www.raintreepublishers.co.uk
Visit our website to find out more information about **Raintree** books.

To order:
☎ Phone 44 (0) 1865 888112
📄 Send a fax to 44 (0) 1865 314091
💻 Visit the Raintree bookshop at **www.raintreepublishers.co.uk** to browse our catalogue and order online.

First published in Great Britain by Raintree, Halley Court, Jordan Hill, Oxford OX2 8EJ, part of Harcourt Education.
Raintree is a registered trademark of Harcourt Education Ltd.

Editorial: Lucy Thunder and Harriet Milles
Design: Michelle Lisseter, Carolyn Gibson and Philippa Baile
Illustrations: Philippa Baile
Picture Research: Melissa Allison and Ginny Stroud-Lewis
Production: Camilla Crask

Originated by Dot Gradations Ltd.
Printed and bound in Italy by Printer Trento srl

The paper used to print this book comes from sustainable resources.

ISBN 1 844 21460 5
10 09 08 07 06
10 9 8 7 6 5 4 3 2 1

British Library Cataloguing in Publication Data
Claybourne, Anna
Can You Tell a Skink From a Salamander?: Classification
590.1'2
A full catalogue record for this book is available from the British Library.

Acknowledgements
The publishers would like to thank the following for permission to reproduce photographs: Auscape International p. 21; Corbis p. 29; Corbis pp. 4–5 (Randy Faris), 10–11 (Stephen Frink), 8 (Lynda Richardson), 26–27 (Keren Su); FLPA pp. 22–23 (Fred Bavendam/Minden Pictures), 12 (Claus Meyer/Minden Pictures), 14, 24–25 (Frans Lanting/Minden Pictures), 18 (Roger Wilmshurst); Getty/PhotoDisk p. 6; Image Quest Marine p. 13 (Jim Greenfield 2004); Natural Visions p. 16 (Heather Angel); Nature Picture Library p. 9 (Doug Wechsler); NHPA pp. 19 (Anthony Bannister), 20–21 (Stephen Dalton), 15 (Roger Tidman); Oxford Scientific Films p. 17 (Norman Helen).

Cover photograph of an Ensatina Salamander, reproduced with permission of FLPA/Minden Pictures/Frans Lanting.

The publishers would like to thank Nancy Harris and Harold Pratt for their assistance in the preparation of this book.

Every effort has been made to contact copyright holders of any material reproduced in this book. Any omissions will be rectified in subsequent printings if notice is given to the publishers.

Contents

Some words are printed in bold, **like this**. You can find out what they mean on page 30. You can also look in the box at the bottom of the page where they first appear.

Which is which?

You are swimming in a warm blue ocean, under a sunny sky. You decide to go back to the beach for a cool drink. You turn around. You see a dark, razor-sharp fin slicing through the water. What is it?

Uh-oh ... what is ▶ that? Can you tell? Is it a dolphin? Or is it something more dangerous?

It could be a dangerous great white shark. Or it could be a harmless basking shark. Perhaps it is not a shark at all. It could be a friendly dolphin.

Being able to tell living things apart is useful for swimmers. It is also an important part of science. It is called **classification**. Classification is all about sorting living things into different groups. These groups are called "classes".

dolphin

shark

Which is which?

*The shape of a living thing can help scientists decide what it is. For example, a dolphin's **dorsal fin** is curved. A shark's is straighter.*

5

classification sorting out living things into groups and types
dorsal fin fin on an animal's back

The science of sorting out

How many different types of living things do you think there are? Hundreds? Thousands?

In fact, there are millions. Scientists have already discovered around 2 million types, or **species** of living things. They are still finding new ones every day. They **classify** them, or sort them out into groups. This makes species easier to study.

Species names

Each species has its own scientific name in Latin. This is so all scientists can use it. For example, the tiger's scientific name is Panthera tigris.

classify	to sort living things into groups and types
invertebrate	animal with no backbone
species	name for a type of living thing
vertebrate	animal with a backbone

But some living things are clever. They can fool you! They look as if they should belong to one group. In fact they are classified into a completely different group. How do these animals do this? Read on to find out!

Living Things
There are many types of living things. Plants and animals are two different types.

Plants
Plants are mainly green, and usually have roots that hold them in one place.

 Grass

 Trees

 Seaweed

Animals
There are two main types of animals.

Invertebrates
Invertebrates are animals that do not have backbones.

 Jellyfish

 Spider

 Crab

Vertebrates
Vertebrates have skeletons and backbones. There are five main types of vertebrates.

 Fish

 Birds

 Mammals

 Amphibians

 Reptiles

Can you tell a skink from a salamander?

They are both smooth and shiny. They both have four legs, long tails, and bright colours. They are both **vertebrates** too. This means they have backbones. But skinks and salamanders belong to completely different animal families.

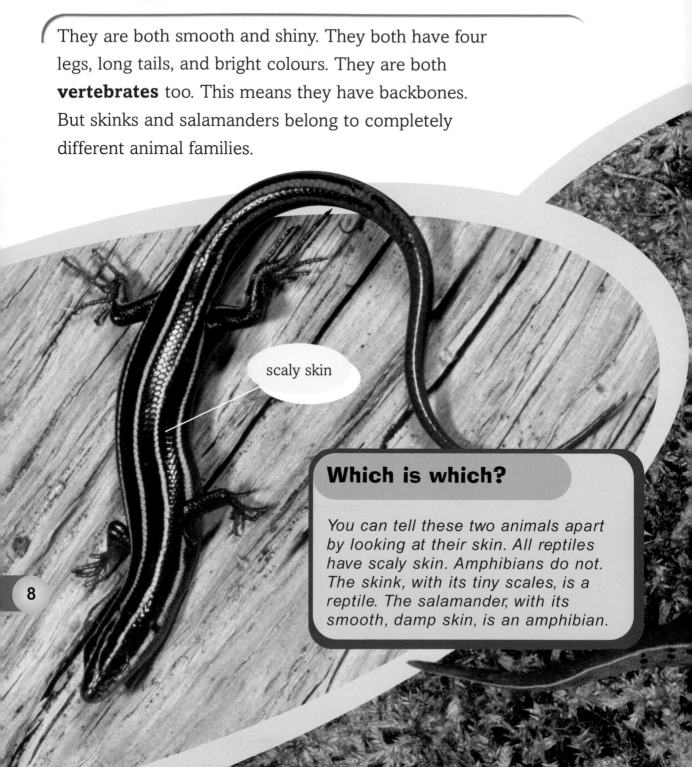

scaly skin

Which is which?

You can tell these two animals apart by looking at their skin. All reptiles have scaly skin. Amphibians do not. The skink, with its tiny scales, is a reptile. The salamander, with its smooth, damp skin, is an amphibian.

A skink is a lizard, a type of **reptile**. Reptiles have scaly skin. Most live on land. Some, like crocodiles and turtles, spend a lot of time in the water.

A salamander is an **amphibian**. Frogs and toads are also amphibians. Amphibians can breathe in air and underwater.

Animal

Vertebrate

Amphibian

Salamander

Reptile

Skink

smooth skin

amphibian   type of animal that can breathe in air and water
reptile   type of animal with scaly skin

Can you tell a bull shark from a dolphin?

These two creatures have almost the same body shape. They are long, narrow, and sleek. They are perfect for sliding through the ocean. They are both **vertebrates** because they have backbones. But there is a big difference between them.

Like all other sharks, bull sharks are **fish**. All fish breathe underwater, using their **gills**.

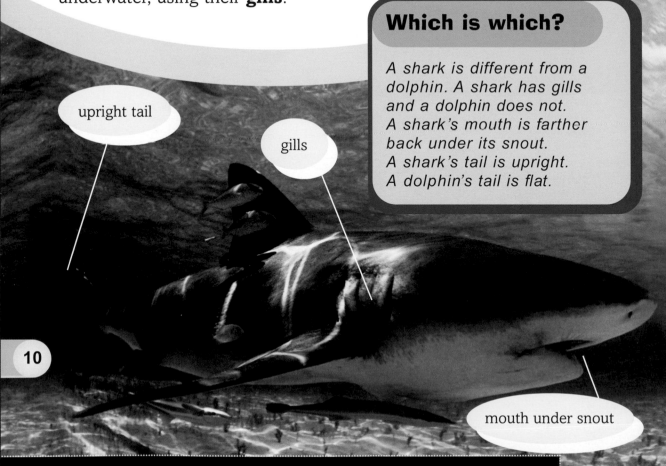

upright tail

gills

mouth under snout

Which is which?

A shark is different from a dolphin. A shark has gills and a dolphin does not. A shark's mouth is farther back under its snout. A shark's tail is upright. A dolphin's tail is flat.

fish	type of animal that swims and breathes in water using gills
gills	body parts that fish use for breathing underwater
mammal	warm-blooded animal that feeds its young on milk

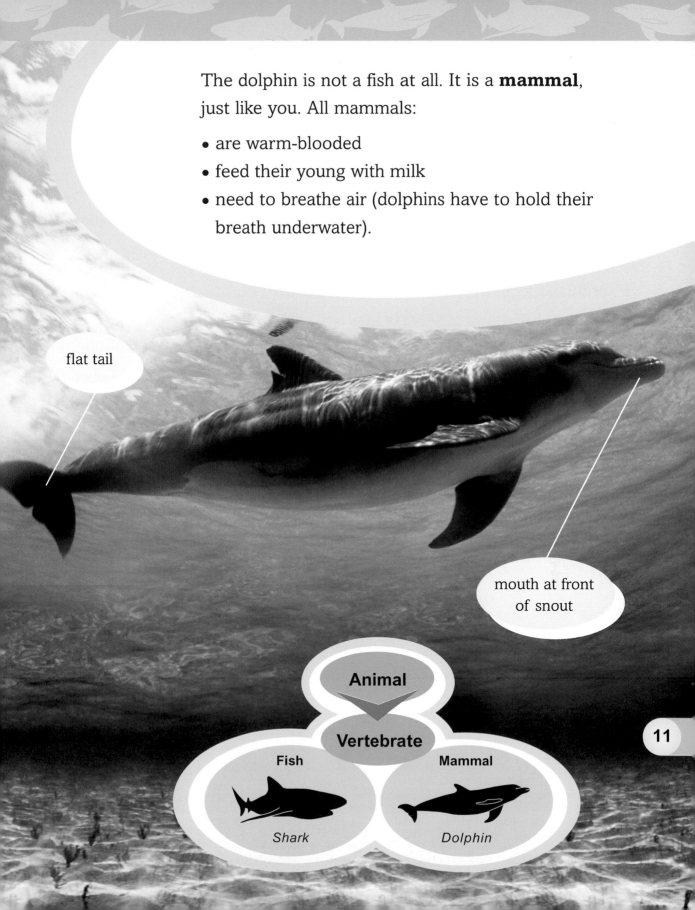

The dolphin is not a fish at all. It is a **mammal**, just like you. All mammals:

- are warm-blooded
- feed their young with milk
- need to breathe air (dolphins have to hold their breath underwater).

flat tail

mouth at front of snout

Animal

Vertebrate

Fish

Shark

Mammal

Dolphin

Can you tell a tarantula from a spider crab?

At first glance, you might think that both of these creatures are spiders. But they are not. They both have eight legs. But they have very different lifestyles.

Tarantulas are spiders. They belong to an **invertebrate** group called **arachnids**. Invertebrates do not have backbones. Arachnids live on land. They usually live in burrows. Tarantulas make strong, stretchy spider silk.

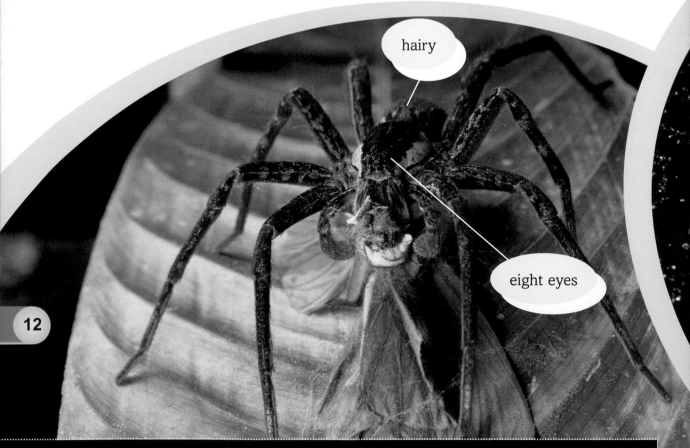

hairy

eight eyes

12

arachnids   group of invertebrate animals with eight legs and a body in two parts
crustaceans   group of invertebrate animals with shells that usually live in water

The spider crab is a type of crab. It lives on the seabed. Crabs belong to an invertebrate group called **crustaceans**. All crustaceans have shells. Most live in the sea and can breathe underwater.

Which is which?

Spiders are hairier than crabs. They have two body sections. Crabs have a hard, smooth shell. Spiders do not. Crabs have two eyes. Spiders have up to eight eyes!

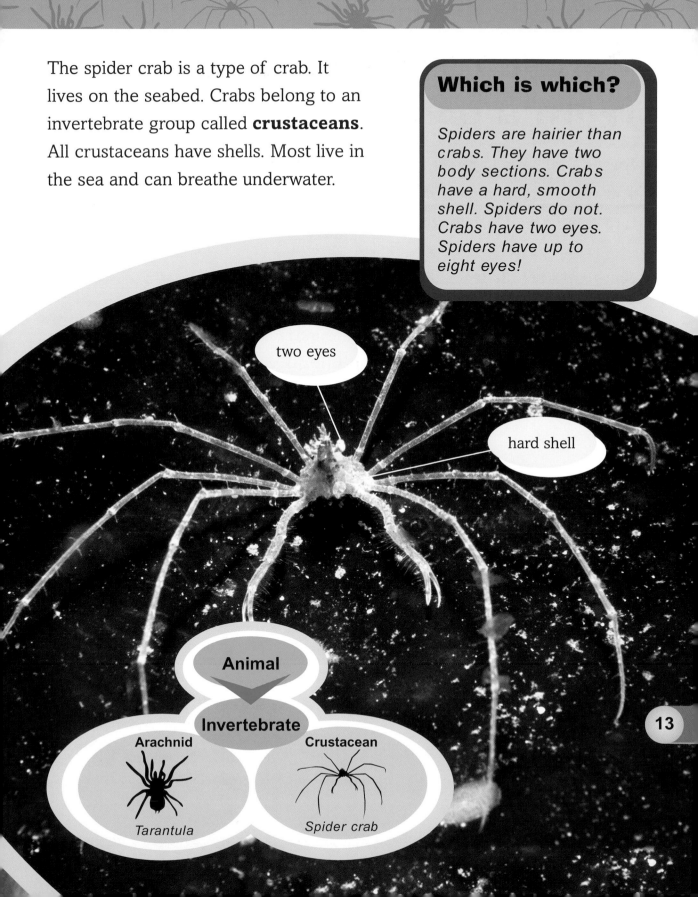

two eyes

hard shell

Animal

Invertebrate

Arachnid

Crustacean

Tarantula

Spider crab

13

Can you tell a flying fox from a golden eagle?

A flying fox gets its name because of its fox-like face. If you saw one flapping past, you might think it was a large bird. But in fact, a flying fox is a type of bat.

Birds are **vertebrate** animals. This means they have backbones. They have feathers and lay eggs. Bats are often mistaken for birds as they fly around. But they do not have feathers. Bats are furry **mammals**. Like other mammals, the flying fox gives birth to live young.

pointed claws

stretched skin

fur

14

feathers

Which is which?

Look at the wings to tell a golden eagle from a bat. Birds have feathery wings. Bats' wings are made of stretched skin. Look for the pointed claws along the edge of a bat's wing.

Animal

Vertebrate

Bird

Golden eagle

Mammal

Flying fox

15

Can you tell a sea anemone from a gerbera?

The two creatures on these pages both look like flowers. But only one of them is a flower.

The creature on this page is an animal called a sea anemone. It belongs to a group of **invertebrates** called **polyps**. Invertebrates do not have backbones. The sea anemone uses its fleshy tentacles to pull in small sea creatures to eat.

The red creature on the opposite page is a plant called a gerbera. If you looked underneath the gerbera, you would see that it has a stem and leaves. It also has roots growing into the ground.

tentacles

mouth

polyps   group of simple, tube-shaped invertebrate animals

Which is which?

How can you tell a plant from an animal? Plants do not have mouths. They do not eat in the same way animals do. They make food in their leaves, using sunlight.

stem

Animal

Invertebrate

Polyps

Sea anemone

Plant

Flowering plant

Gerbera

Can you tell an eel from a sea snake?

These long, skinny animals both live in the sea. Eels look like snakes, but in fact they are a type of **fish**. Just like other fish, they have fins. They breathe underwater, using **gills**. The eel in this photo has been caught by a fisherman.

gills

fin

Which is which?

Almost all fish have fins – even eels, though theirs are long and narrow. Snakes never have fins. So you can spot the fish here by looking for a fin.

Sea snakes are **reptiles**, like other snakes. Sea snakes live in the sea and swim by rippling their bodies from side to side. Unlike fish, they do not have fins. They cannot breathe underwater. They have to come to the surface to breathe.

There is another difference too. The common eel is harmless. But yellow-bellied sea snakes have the deadliest poison of any snake.

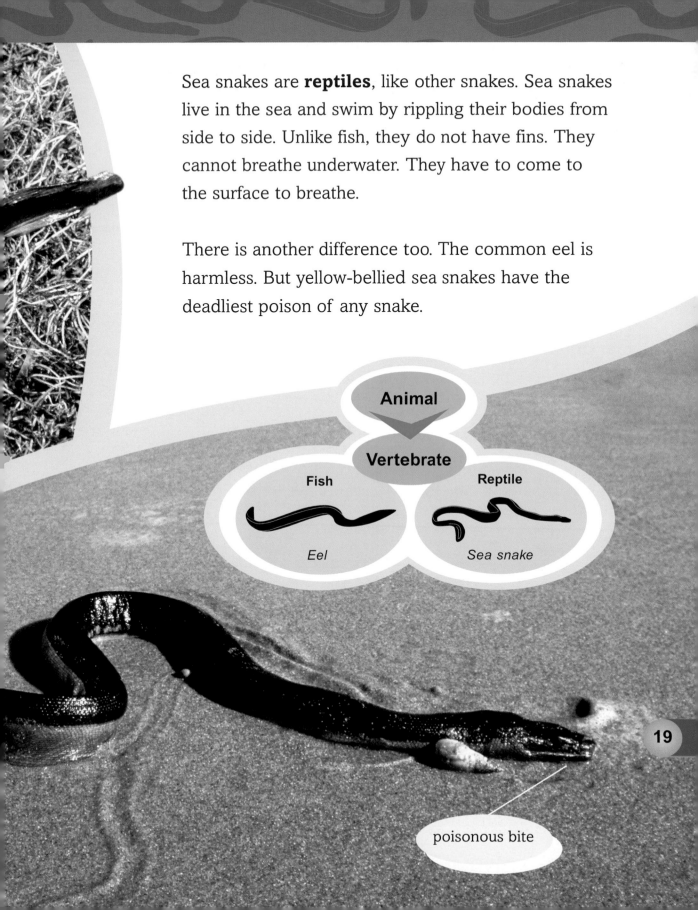

Animal

Vertebrate

Fish

Eel

Reptile

Sea snake

poisonous bite

Can you tell a fluffy glider from a flying squirrel?

You are walking in a forest. You see a small, grey, furry animal gliding through the air. Its stretched-out skin acts like wings. What is it? Well, it depends where you are.

In Australia, you would probably be looking at a fluffy glider. The fluffy glider belongs to a group of **mammals** called **marsupials**. Female marsupials carry their young in a pouch on their bellies. Kangaroos are also marsupials.

In Canada, the animal would be a flying squirrel. The flying squirrel belongs to a group of mammals called **rodents**. Rodents are small, covered in fur, and have long teeth.

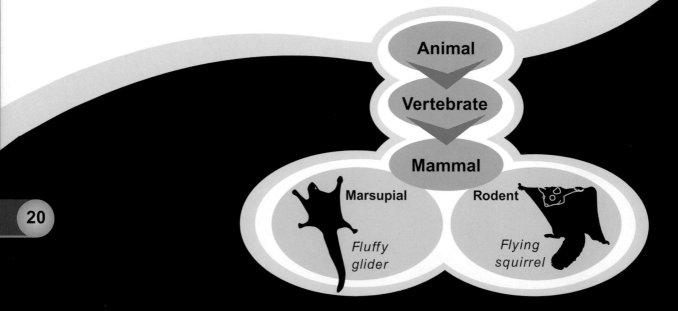

Animal

Vertebrate

Mammal

Marsupial

Rodent

Fluffy glider

Flying squirrel

marsupial   type of mammal that often carries its young in a pouch
rodent   type of small furry mammal with long teeth

Which is which?

It is hard to tell these animals apart. The fluffy glider has a longer tail. You may be able to spot a female marsupial by the pouch on its belly.

pouch

long tail

21

Can you tell a leafy sea dragon from seagrass?

The leafy sea dragon has a clever disguise. Its "leafy" fins and frills look just like seagrass, a kind of sea plant.

This disguise is very good **camouflage** for the sea dragon. The sea dragon is a type of **fish**. Camouflage helps it to sneak up on its **prey** without being spotted.

Which is which?

To tell a fish from a plant, see if it has a head and a face. The sea dragon has a dragon-like head at one end. Plants do not have heads. If a creature is rooted into the soil or seabed, it is probably a plant, not an animal.

head

face

camouflage	patterns and shapes that blend in with the surroundings
prey	animals that get eaten by other animals

Sea dragons may look leafy and like a plant. But they can move around to look for food.

Seagrass is a type of plant. Unlike most animals, plants do not have brains or eyes. They cannot walk or swim around. Unlike animals, most plants have roots.

Animal

Vertebrate

Fish

Sea dragon

Plant

Flowering plant

Seagrass

Can you tell a bonobo from a human?

You can tell the difference at once, can't you? The bonobo is much hairier. He has longer arms and his face is a different shape.

This is a bonobo ▶
called Kanzi, with his human teacher, Sue Savage-Rumbaugh.

Which is which?

You can tell humans apart from other apes by the way they talk. Humans can use lots of words strung together into sentences. This is one of the main things that makes humans different from other animals.

ape	type of clever mammal that can walk on two legs
genes	instructions inside living things that control how they grow

Yet bonobos are very like humans. Bonobos are our closest relatives. The **genes** of humans and bonobos are 99.6 per cent the same.

Humans and bonobos both belong to the highest group of **mammals**. This group is called primates. The group includes humans, monkeys, and **apes**.

Animal

Vertebrate

Mammal

Primate

Human   Bonobo

More to discover

Scientists are always finding new living things – especially small ones, like beetles and bugs. Each new creature has to be sorted into a group, or **classified**.

Sometimes, new **species** do not belong anywhere in the **classification** system. The system has to be changed to fit them in. Other times, scientists cannot decide how to classify something. They may even disagree about this.

▼ *What does this look like to you? Scientists disagreed for a long time about how to classify the panda.*

26

The giant panda is an example. Long ago, people thought the panda was related to big cats. Then it was classified with raccoons.

Then, scientists changed their minds. They decided the panda was a kind of bear. As scientists learn more, they often need to change the way they classify things.

27

Classification made easy

Living things are divided into five main groups, or kingdoms:

- Monera (e.g. bacteria. Some bacteria can make you sick.)
- Protista (e.g. algae, a simple plant that grows in water)
- Fungi (e.g. mushrooms)
- Plants
- Animals

In this book, we have looked at the kingdoms of plants and animals. The diagram below will remind you how these work.

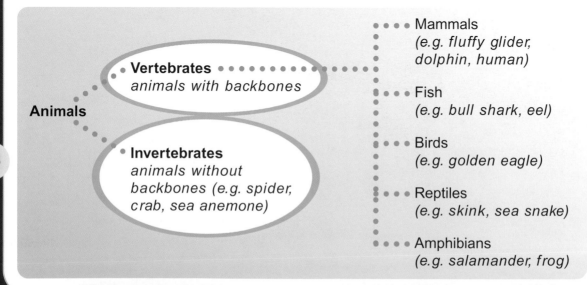

Plants

Flowering plants
(e.g. gerbera. Plants that can carry water from their roots to their other parts)

Non-flowering plants

Simple plants
(e.g. moss)

Animals

Vertebrates
animals with backbones

Invertebrates
animals without backbones (e.g. spider, crab, sea anemone)

Mammals
(e.g. fluffy glider, dolphin, human)

Fish
(e.g. bull shark, eel)

Birds
(e.g. golden eagle)

Reptiles
(e.g. skink, sea snake)

Amphibians
(e.g. salamander, frog)

Classification quiz

Now it is your turn to be a scientist. Can you **classify** these sea creatures from their pictures and descriptions? Where would you put each one in the diagram opposite?

1. Penguin
Two flippers and two legs • Swims underwater • Breathes air • Covered in oily feathers

2. Octopus
Eight legs • Two eyes • Soft, rubbery body, with no bones • Lives in the sea

3. Stingray
Wide, aeroplane-like shape with two wings • Long tail • Lives in the sea • Breathes underwater • Has tough, smooth skin • Has a skeleton and a backbone

Answers

1. It must be a *bird*. Only birds have feathers.

2. With no bones at all, it has to be an *invertebrate*.

3. It is a *fish*. Only fish have backbones, live in the sea, and can breathe underwater.

Glossary

amphibian type of animal that can breathe in air and water. Frogs, toads, and salamanders are all amphibians.

ape type of clever mammal that can walk on two legs. Humans, bonobos, and chimpanzees are all apes.

arachnids group of invertebrate animals with eight legs and a body in two parts. Arachnids can spin silk.

camouflage patterns and shapes that blend in with the surroundings. Camouflage helps living things to hide from their enemies.

classification sorting out living things into groups and types.

classify to sort living things out into groups and types. Scientists classify each new living thing they discover.

crustaceans group of invertebrate animals with shells that usually live in water. Crabs, shrimps, and lobsters are crustaceans.

dorsal fin fin on an animal's back. Sharks and most other fish, whales, and dolphins have dorsal fins.

fish type of animal that swims and breathes in water using gills. Sharks are fish.

genes instructions inside living things that control how they grow. Each species of living thing has its own special pattern of genes.

gills body parts that fish use for breathing underwater. A fish's gills are on the sides of its neck.

invertebrate animal with no backbone. Snails and spiders are invertebrates.

mammal warm-blooded animal that feeds its young on milk. Humans, mice, dogs, and cats are mammals.

marsupial type of mammal that often carries its young in a pouch. Kangaroos are marsupials.

polyps group of simple, tube-shaped invertebrate animals. A sea anemone is a type of polyp.

prey animals that get eaten by other animals. For example, tigers hunt prey such as deer and wild pigs.

reptile type of animal with scaly skin. Snakes, lizards, and crocodiles are reptiles.

rodent type of small, furry mammal with long teeth. Mice, rats, and squirrels are rodents.

species name for a type of living thing. Members of the same species can breed and have babies together.

vertebrate animal with a backbone. Tigers, fish, and humans are vertebrates.

Want to know more?

Books to read

• *Living Things: Classification*, by Anita Ganeri (Heinemann Library, 2002)

• *The Wild World of the Future*, by Claire Pye (Firefly Books Ltd, 2003)

• *Weird Animals*, by Bobbie Kalman (Crabtree Publishing, 1995)

Places to visit

• Melbourne Zoo
  Elliot Avenue,
  Parkville,
  Victoria 3052
  Australia
  www.zoo.org.au

• The Natural History Museum
  Cromwell Road,
  London SW7 5BD
  www.nhm.ac.uk

Websites

• www.amonline.net.au/research/index.cfm
  A website that includes lots of facts about animal classification.

• www.museums.org.za/bio/
  A site about the many types of animals that live in South Africa.

Want to know how animals are built and how they can do amazing feats? Check out *Super-flea*.

Animals survive by eating other animals and plants. To see how this works, read *Shark Snacks*.

Index